NATIONAL GEOGRAPHIC

Ladders

It's a Home Run!

Take Me Out to the BALL GAME

words by Jack Norworth
music by Albert Von Tilzer

In many ballparks, it's a **tradition** to sing "Take Me Out to the Ball Game" during the seventh-inning stretch. Most fans can sing along with the **refrain.** Did you know there are two **verses,** too? The verses and the refrain tell a story about Katie Casey, a girl who loves baseball, America's **national pastime.**

REFRAIN

Take me out to the ball game,
Take me out with the crowd.
Buy me some peanuts and Cracker Jack,
I don't care if I never get back,
Let me root, root, root for the home team,
If they don't win it's a shame.
For it's one, two, three strikes, you're out,
At the old ball game.

root cheer
sou a small amount of money
beau boyfriend

VERSE 1

Katie Casey was baseball mad.
Had the fever and had it bad;
Just to root for the hometown crew,
Ev'ry sou Katie blew.
On a Saturday, her young beau
Called to see if she'd like to go,
To see a show but Miss Kate said,
"No, I'll tell you what you can do."

VERSE 2

Katie Casey saw all the games,
Knew the players by their first names;
Told the umpire he was wrong,
All along good and strong.
When the score was just two to two,
Katie Casey knew what to do,
Just to cheer up the boys she knew,
She made the gang sing this song:

MIKE KELLY.

BOSTON

WORK AND WI

FRED FEARNOT'S STEAL TO

Check In How would you describe Katie Casey?

The Old Ball Game

by Michael Bilski

BASEBALL IS BORN

Americans have enjoyed baseball since the early 1800s. It grew so popular that it became known as America's **national pastime.**

The basic rules of baseball were set by Alexander Cartwright and the New York Knickerbocker Base Ball Club in 1845. Before then, players could hit a runner with the ball to make an out. Ouch! Although the Knickerbockers made the rules, they lost the first game they played with the new rules. The score was 23 to 1!

When baseball first began, teams played for fun and were not paid. Over time that changed. In 1869, the Cincinnati Red Stockings became the first professional team to pay all its players. Soon, professional leagues arose.

1846

The Knickerbockers play the first baseball game using the new rules in Hoboken, New Jersey.

Elysian Fields in Hoboken, New Jersey

1866

The first women's baseball team is started at Vassar College.

1845

Alexander Cartwright and the Knickerbockers list the rules of baseball.

Alexander Cartwright

1869

The Cincinnati Red Stockings, the first all-professional team, play their first game.

The Cincinnati Red Stockings, 1869

1876
The National League is formed.

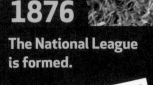

William Hulbert, founder of the National League

IT'S IN THE CARDS

As baseball grew, so did baseball **traditions.** The tradition of collecting cards began in the 1860s. In the 1870s, companies created baseball cards. Decades later, the Topps Chewing Gum Company sold packs of gum with baseball cards inside.

Most fans today collect baseball cards for fun. Some people, though, collect baseball cards for their value. A rare 1909 card showing future Hall of Fame player Honus Wagner sold for $2,800,000 in 2007. Hold on to those cards!

MIKE KELLY.

Baseball cards, late 1800s

1884

Moses Fleetwood Walker becomes the first African American player in the major leagues.

MOSES FLEETWOOD WALKER

In 1884, Moses Fleetwood Walker became the first African American player to play baseball in a major league. He played for the Toledo Blue Stockings, which was a major league team then. A long time passed before another African American followed in Walker's footsteps.

1900

The American League is formed.

1887

Goodwin and Company makes the first widely distributed set of baseball cards.

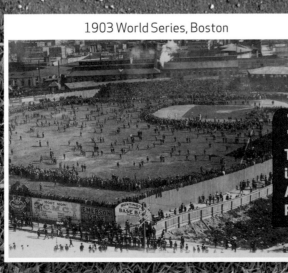

1903 World Series, Boston

1903

The first World Series is played. The Boston Americans defeat the Pittsburgh Pirates.

1907

Alta Weiss becomes the first professional woman baseball player.

Alta Weiss

1908

"Take Me Out to the Ball Game" is written.

1909

The famous Honus Wagner baseball card is printed.

BASEBALL CATCHES ON

The publication of "Take Me Out to the Ball Game" in 1908 meant baseball was a hit with the public. Who knew we would still be singing the song more than one hundred years later? Fans continue the tradition of singing "Take Me Out to the Ball Game" at many ballparks during the seventh-inning stretch. Singing along unites the fans and supports the home team.

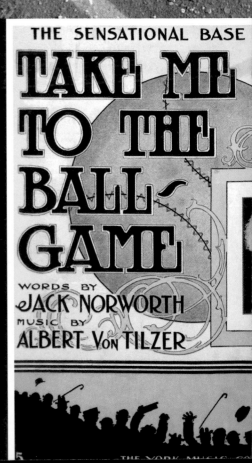

THE SENSATIONAL BASE

TAKE ME TO THE BALL GAME

WORDS BY JACK NORWORTH
MUSIC BY ALBERT VON TILZER

THE CEREMONIAL FIRST PITCH

In 1910, President Taft began a baseball tradition. He threw the ball onto the field at the first game of the season. This started a tradition of presidents, other elected officials, and celebrities throwing the "ceremonial first pitch." Since 1910, all presidents except for Jimmy Carter have taken part in this **ceremony.** Carter may have been too busy for baseball while president, but he went to many games after leaving office.

President Taft on opening day, 1910

1910
President Taft throws the ceremonial first pitch on opening day.

1916
The Cleveland Indians become the first major league team with numbers on uniforms.

1917

The United States enters World War I.

1918

The "Star-Spangled Banner" is sung at a baseball game.

1919

Scandal! Reports say eight Chicago White Sox players take bribes and lose the World Series on purpose.

THE BATTLE BEYOND THE BALLPARK

In April of 1917, the United States entered World War I. Many baseball players joined the military. As the war went on, a new musical tradition began. At the 1918 World Series, a military band played "The Star-Spangled Banner" during the seventh-inning stretch to honor military servicemen. After that, the song was played at every World Series game and every season opener. During World War II, this tradition changed. "The Star-Spangled Banner" was played before every game instead. That tradition continues today.

Players stand at attention for "The Star-Spangled Banner."

National League All-Star Team, 1933

Official Score Book
Comiskey Park
BASE BALL PALACE OF THE WORLD
10¢
SEASON OF NINETEEN THIRTY-THREE
always a hit
BLUE VALLEY BUTTER
finer flavor

LOOK AT ALL THE STARS!

One of baseball's yearly traditions is the Major League All-Star Game. It is called the "Midsummer Classic" because it is played in July. The first All-Star Game was played in July 1933 at Comiskey Park in Chicago. Baseball managers and fans chose stars from the American and National Leagues to play. It has become a tradition for fans to vote for their favorite players for each year's game. The voting lets the fans see the stars gather on the same field.

1921
A baseball game is broadcast on radio for the first time.

1931
The Baseball Writers' Association begins a tradition. It names a "most valuable player" for each league.

1933
The first Major League All-Star Game is played.

1939
The National Baseball Hall of Fame and Museum opens.

1935
In Cincinnati, the first night game takes place.

1941
The United States enters World War II.

The girls' league in action

A HALL FOR BALL

The National Baseball Hall of Fame and Museum opened in 1939 in Cooperstown, New York. Each year, players are **inducted** into the Hall. The candidates must have played within the last 20 years and have been retired for 5 years. They also must have played in the major leagues for at least 10 years. Those who receive at least 75 percent of the votes are inducted in a ceremony. Only the best make it. At the induction ceremony, each new member is honored with a plaque. Broadcasters, umpires, and managers, among others, are elected separately.

The National Baseball Hall of Fame and Museum

LET'S GO, LADIES!

From the start, professional baseball was a man's sport. During World War II, many baseball players joined the military. Baseball team owners didn't have enough male players to draw crowds. So in 1943, the All-American Girls Professional Baseball League was formed. It started with just four teams, but there were ten teams during one season. The women drew crowds of as many as 10,000 people per game. The league even had its own victory song. Although the league ended in 1954, the players were pioneers for the girls and women playing today.

1942

President Roosevelt gives baseball the "green light" to continue during the war.

1941-45

More than 500 players serve in World War II.

1943

The All-American Girls Professional Baseball League is formed.

1947

Jackie Robinson becomes the first African American player in the major leagues since 1884.

ROGER MARIS

In 1961, Roger Maris hit his 61st home run, but fans weren't happy. Maris had broken Babe Ruth's 1927 record of 60 home runs in a season. Ruth was a legendary player, and fans didn't want Maris to defeat his record. Some claimed Maris didn't actually break Babe Ruth's record. Ruth's record was set in a 154-game season, but Maris's was set in a 162-game season. In 1961, Maris was also voted the American League's Most Valuable Player and helped the Yankees win the World Series.

1947

The World Series is broadcast on TV for the first time.

LONG STREAKS

Joe DiMaggio

Fans are excited by record-setting long streaks. Joe DiMaggio had hits in 56 games in a row in 1941! Pete Rose's 44-game hitting streak in 1978 is the closest to that. Lou Gehrig played 2,130 games in a row for the New York Yankees. His record lasted for 56 years until Cal Ripken, Jr. broke it in 1995. Ripken played in 2,632 games between May 30, 1982 and September 20, 1998.

1958

The New York Giants and Brooklyn Dodgers move to California. They become the first major league teams west of St. Louis.

1965

The first indoor game is played. It is in the Houston Astrodome.

1961

Roger Maris hits 61 home runs. He breaks Babe Ruth's single-season record set in 1927.

CELEBRATING A HERO

On April 15, 1947, Jackie Robinson of the Brooklyn Dodgers became the first African American player in a major league since 1884. A new tradition began in 2004 when Major League Baseball began to celebrate Jackie Robinson Day. At ballparks on April 15, every player, manager, coach, and umpire wears Jackie's number, 42. On all other days no one is allowed to wear that number.

1972
Roberto Clemente dies in a plane crash.

1973
The American League begins to use the designated hitter rule.

ROBERTO CLEMENTE

From 1955 to 1972, the Pittsburgh Pirates had a great outfielder, Roberto Clemente. He was known for his baseball skills and for his work helping people in need. Clemente died in a plane crash while taking supplies to earthquake survivors in Nicaragua in 1972. He was inducted into the Hall of Fame the next year. Usually a player could not be inducted until five years after the end of his baseball career. This rule was changed for Clemente because of the great things he did. Clemente was also the first Latin American player to be inducted.

1974
Hank Aaron breaks Babe Ruth's career home run record.

2004

Jackie Robinson Day is celebrated for the first time.

2000

The Major League Baseball season opens in Japan for the first time.

1997

Jackie Robinson's number 42 is retired.

WHAT'S NEXT?

Think about what baseball was like in the 1840s, and then picture baseball today. A lot has changed! Rules have been established. Professional leagues have grown. Traditions have developed to celebrate important events. Records have been made and broken. Players from different backgrounds have become part of the game. Now imagine the future. What's next for baseball?

Check In   Who has played an important role in the history of baseball? How?

BASEBALL
AROUND THE WORLD

by Michael Bilski

Baseball started in the United States and became a **national pastime.** Soon it spread to other countries, especially in Latin America and Asia. Whatever you call it—*béisbol*, *besuboru*, or *baseball*—it's an international sport with great players around the world.

National Baseball Hall of Fame and Museum Cooperstown, New York

ROD CAREW
Panama

HARRY WRIGHT
England

LUIS APARICIO
Venezuela

JUAN MARICHAL
Dominican Republic

ROBERTO ALOMAR
Puerto Rico

Famous Players

Players come from many countries to play on major league teams in the U.S. Some of the best are honored in the Baseball Hall of Fame and Museum. The Hall has nine players (shown below) from other countries. In the future, we're sure to see Hall of Famers from many more places.

Halls of Fame

Other countries besides the U.S. have halls of fame, too.

- The Japanese Baseball Hall of Fame and Museum opened in 1959. Trophies from the World Baseball Classic are displayed there.
- The *Salón de la Fama y Museo del Béisbol Venezolano* opened in 1953 in Valencia, Venezuela. It's in a huge shopping mall, and the building is shaped like a baseball diamond.
- The *Salón de la Fama del Béisbol Cubano* opened in 1939 in Cuba.
- The Korean Baseball Hall of Fame opened in 1995. It has a library with 2,000 baseball books and 800 baseball films.

TONY PEREZ
Cuba

ROBERTO CLEMENTE
Puerto Rico

ORLANDO CEPEDA
Puerto Rico

FERGUSON JENKINS
Canada

THE WORLD BASEBALL CLASSIC

The World Baseball Classic (WBC) is an international competition that was held in 2006 and 2009. It will be held again in 2013. Sixteen of the countries below will compete. Teams must **qualify** to compete. Teams from the countries in red have competed successfully in the WBC before. Those teams already qualify. Teams from the countries in orange must qualify to compete.

1. AUSTRALIA
2. CHINA
3. CUBA
4. DOMINICAN REPUBLIC
5. ITALY
6. JAPAN
7. MEXICO
8. NETHERLANDS
9. PUERTO RICO
10. SOUTH KOREA

11. UNITED STATES
12. VENEZUELA
13. CANADA
14. CHINESE TAIPEI (TAIWAN)
15. PANAMA
16. SOUTH AFRICA
17. BRAZIL
18. COLOMBIA
19. CZECH REPUBLIC
20. FRANCE

21. GERMANY
22. GREAT BRITAIN
23. ISRAEL
24. NEW ZEALAND
25. NICARAGUA
26. SPAIN
27. PHILIPPINES
28. THAILAND

The World Baseball Classic

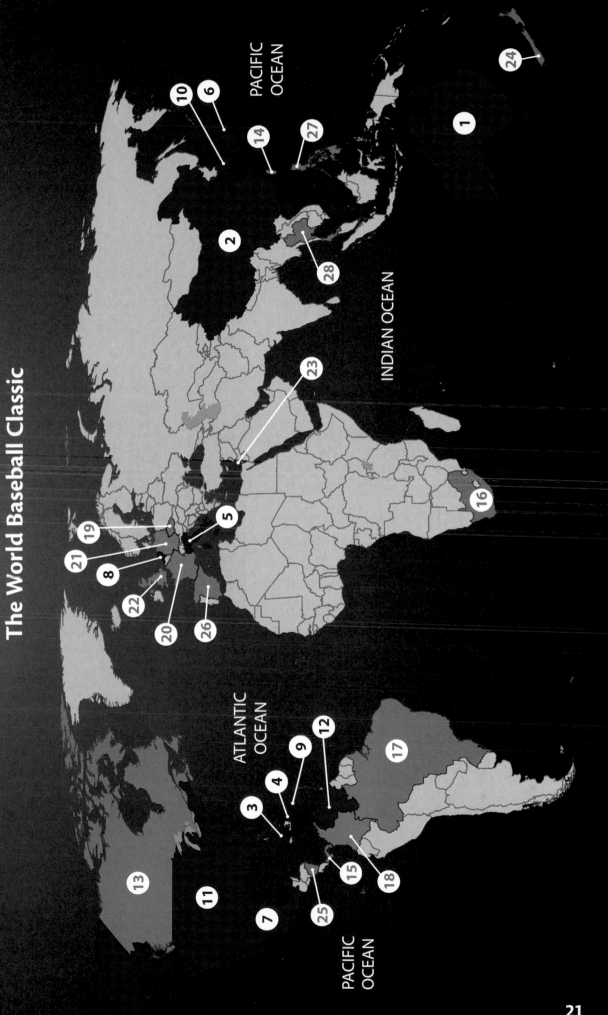

PACIFIC OCEAN

ATLANTIC OCEAN

INDIAN OCEAN

PACIFIC OCEAN

A World Tour

Let's look at a few countries around the world where professional baseball is played. The rules may be the same, but baseball **traditions** are influenced by the history and culture of each country.

ASIA

Japan

besuboru = baseball in Japanese

In the 1870s an American professor in Tokyo introduced baseball to the Japanese. Since then, baseball has become Japan's most popular team sport. Fans there are very enthusiastic. During the game, fans take part in organized cheers along with the cheerleaders. It's a tradition in some ballparks to release balloons during the seventh-inning stretch.

Japan won first place in both the 2006 and 2009 World Baseball Classic.

SOUTH AMERICA

Venezuela

béisbol = baseball in Spanish

College students returning to Venezuela from the U.S. brought baseball to Venezuela in the late 1800s. While soccer is the most popular sport in most of Latin America, baseball dominates in Venezuela. The U.S. has a tradition of eating hot dogs at a ball game, but fans in Venezuela are likely to eat *arepas*. These are a type of cornbread with fillings such as ham and cheese.

Venezuela captured third place in the 2009 World Baseball Classic.

THE CARIBBEAN

Dominican Republic

béisbol = baseball in Spanish

Americans taught baseball to Cubans in the 1860s. Later the Cubans taught it to the Dominicans. Now baseball is the national sport of the Dominican Republic. More U.S. major league players come from the D.R. than from any other foreign country. Many excited fans attend games with painted faces, flags, and noisemakers. Hungry fans can buy rice with beans at the ballpark.

In the 2006 World Baseball Classic, the Dominican Republic won fifth place.

EUROPE

Netherlands

honkbal = baseball in Dutch

In 1911, a Dutchman visited the U.S. and brought home the game of baseball. The Netherlands likes baseball more than any other European country. Even so, soccer still has more fans. In fact, one reason people there like baseball is because it is played between soccer seasons.

The Netherlands came in seventh place in the 2009 World Baseball Classic.

Check In Outside of the U.S., where is baseball the most popular?

Discuss Events and Time Lines

1. In what order is the information organized in "The Old Ball Game"? Why do you think it is organized in this way?

2. Choose an event in baseball that interests you. Explain what happened.

3. Choose a tradition in baseball. How do you think it helps players or fans?

4. In which baseball tradition would you most like to participate? Why?